The information in this book is not intended to diagnose or treat any concerns, nor is it intended as a substitute for proper professional help. Each individual's health concerns, whether mental or physical, should be evaluated by a qualified professional.

It is the author's opinion that books such as these can provide a positive support system for those going through difficult times. However, each individual is different and such differences must be taken into consideration.

If you or someone you know is in crisis, please contact a crisis line in your area. Go to: http://suicidehotlines.com/ or call:
1-800-SUICIDE (1-800-784-2433)
or 1-800-273-TALK (1-800-273-8255).

Please get help, whether for yourself or someone you care about.

ISBN
978-0-557-94013-4

Acknowledgements:

There are so many people that have contributed to this book. In fact, it may be said that everyone in my life has contributed in their own fashion. Of course, there are a few who stand out a bit from the rest.

I'd like to thank **Roy Edmunson** *who created the artwork for this book. The unique mandalas and cover art are all his work.*

I met both **JeanPaul M. John** *and* **Tanya Brown** *through the Mental Health site on Facebook. They provided a great deal of motivation and encouragement, as did the fans on that site.*

Of everyone I know, my greatest fan is **Adam Seitz**, *my best friend who always loves what I write and helps me each and every day.*

I'd also like to thank **Mrs. Eliot**, *my 2nd grade teacher who first taught me that I had a talent;* **Mr. Garnet**, *my 9th grade English teacher for teaching me I was capable of more, and* **Mrs. Harder**, *another teacher who truly gave me the dream of becoming an author.*

Finally, I'd like to thank **myself** *for surviving, for never giving up and for fulfilling one of my biggest dreams – the creation of this book. Eventually we all have to create our own "happily ever after". This is a big part of mine.*

Introduction

I've had one of those lives that seems destined to inspire others. Over and over again I've faced new battles and yet somehow I've managed to conquer every one of them.

It is my sincere hope that those who open these pages and read the words inside will feel themselves uplifted and encouraged. I truly know what the dark times of the soul can do to a person, but I also know that we each have the ability to rise above and come out of the darkness into a new world of wonderful possibilities.

After each of these poems, I've written a small piece about how each came to be. I often wonder what factors drove the great authors I so admire to write their masterpieces, and I feel it adds more to the poem to know its origins. I hope you feel the same way.

Most importantly, open your heart, listen with your soul and let these words speak to you. Life is filled with cycles—and though many of them bring pain, all things are temporary. The pain eventually does go away.

Charred

I am Charred…
Burned and Scarred.
The Fires that lit me,
The Flames that bit me—
All the Villains have gone…
And I must Grow…move on.

The embers of my Pain still smoldering…
Yet somehow I must go soldiering on.
The flames reach out to kiss—
My tender branches hiss.

So far I've grown only to decay—
The Fire takes my Growth away.
Fuel for Fire, a Tortured Soul,
Wondering if I'll ever be Whole.
Oh! When will this wretched pain find Peace?
I cry it again…and again…then cease…

Quiet now, I sit and wait,
Knowing not if heat will e'er abate;
Knowing only that Life IS Life—
Filled with tears of joy and strife.
Life IS growth, and so I Fight
To Grow…despite the Fire's light.

Someday…Far away in time,
I will find Peace…Serenity sublime;
And I'll look back at black charred husk
That once did glow like sun at dusk.
My roots reach deep in ashen dirt,
That once was symbol of my hurt –
But now the Richest soil around,
Where Nutrients and Life all abound.

My roots and stem and leaves are strong
Because I fought that Fight so long;
Because I knew that Someday I'd see
A Flameless night…Serenity.

A few years ago I went through a phase where it seemed that every time I grew, it was only fuel for the next fire in my life. Over and over again I felt burned and charred by shadows of the past, and this poem was written in response to that agony.

I can't help but notice that at the end of the poem I held onto hope in a "Someday" that would be more peaceful, and I hope that when you find yourself being burned by life – you too will find a Someday to hang on to.

I dedicate this poem to all of those who reach out with hope for a possible future to help them face their demons from the past.

A Hiccup in Time

The vastness of the Universe surrounds me...
Stretching into Infinity it confounds me.
This Hiccup in Time –
Not one bit Sublime –
Will sometime pass from around me.

My Pain, though great – not Eternal...
And so I often journal,
Remembering when
I used to grin
And felt it all Internal.

Life is a funny little thing,
One moment is cold – the next is Spring.
A reminder to be Grateful,
Never being hateful,
For paupers may become Kings.

Pain hurts – a simple fact,
But someday will forget its act.
Life will get better,
I swear by this letter
And one day my dreams I will attract.

It was one of those flashes of insight, a few minutes where I felt the vastness of the universe, and my problems seemed so small in comparison. It felt so good compared to the pain I had been living in, so I quickly grabbed my pen and paper and wrote this poem, hoping to cling to that moment and never let it go.

The moment eventually passed, of course, but not until after I had written two poems about it that even now give me a glimmer of how it felt.

The cycles of life are strange, indeed, and we never know what's coming next into our lives. One thing is certain, though, and that's change. Every emotion is eventually temporary. Consider that in this moment you may hurt, but who knows what the next will bring?

Each life experience is indeed a hiccup in time – a momentary glimpse of our lives amidst eternity. So when you feel good – hang on to it! Write, talk, sing – whatever you can do to make it last longer; and when you feel bad – remember it's temporary – just like a hiccup.

Peace

A gentle, rolling feeling comes o'er me...
Issues here, but no longer dominant.
My past: painful...but as far as I can see
Completely recoverable and meant
to be.
Before, my stomach knotted, ached;
Shaking hands, shoulders clenched and
throbbing head;
But now a peace o'er comes me, gives me break.
Serenity lies where frustration tread.

Life is strange sometimes, we seldom know why.
Events in past forgotten...Now we cry,
And though we know with every down – an up—
Survival insists we avoid that cup.

To thrive demands a different set of rules—
Demands our Mortal Fears we stand and face.
Though not alone, we're given plenty tools;
If all our inner strength we do embrace.

This sensation never will I forget.
Certain now more in my Future I'll get,
And with that thought I bid you all goodnight.
Sleep well, dream in peace – know that it's all
right.

This is the second of the two poems I wrote during my flash of insight (see *Hiccup in Time*). This one uses exactly 10 syllables on each line to give a sense of purpose and exactness to its message.

It's a simple enough message, but one I still find I get lost in when I read it. What a wonderful feeling to remember that, "*serenity lies where frustration tread*".

Life is filled with events that surprise us years later with emotion, long after we thought we were through. No one wants to deal with the old pains, but if we face them – we can win.

I dedicate this poem to all those who face their mortal fears, who look boldly at the shadows from their past and work to defeat them.

<u>*Now I Lay Me Down to Rest*</u>

Now I lay me down to rest,
Afraid of nightmares and their tests.
The darkest depths within my mind,
Leave me helpless and confined.

I wish and work and nightly pray—
That this time they'll not come my way!
But deep inside I think I know:
The 'mares exist for me to grow.

Please let me grow another way!
Let me wake to bright new day!
Without such torments from my sleep...
When I rest – let it be deep.

But stubborn facts refuse to change
And I am forced to rearrange;
And thus another night I face—
Attempt my fears to erase

What? What is this?
I am awakened by the morn!
Where were terrors in my sleep?
I feel at peace, relaxed, reborn!

We never know on what day
Our Nightmares will simply go away.
And so until then, try to rest,
And go to sleep, despite the tests.

All of my life I've had nightmares, night terrors and other horrible issues in the dark. Some people will never know what courage it takes for some to go to sleep, but I do.

I was talking to a friend about his struggles with sleeping and it inspired me to write this poem. I've found it peaceful to read and comforting to remember its message.

It's normal to base our thoughts of the future on our experiences of the past – what other judge do we have? Unfortunately, this is often inaccurate. We never know what will happen in the next moment and life is nothing if not full of surprises.

I dedicate this poem to all those who understand the courage it takes to go to sleep, and all those that continue to try until they do.

When the Sun Goes Down

One day I ventured through the wooded glade,
Searching for Self, for God, for Destiny
I sat awhile and rested in the shade
Contemplating my long journey thus far

I saw the squirrel gath'ring winter food
I watched the doe teach her fawn to listen
I smiled as I watched the rabbit's large brood
Then slowly got up to begin my walk.

I've walked and crawled and tripped,
for this – my goal
Though others – born with the gifts that I seek
All that I desire is to become whole
A simple thing, but essential to me.

Glancing up at setting sun – am I close?
How can I go on without the Light's aid?
I hurry now, regretting my repose
Did that one break cost me my heart's desire?

The sky explodes in colors bright and I...
I can't help but stare in awe at the sight
But sunset means I'm done – I sob and cry
Was my long walk – my fight all for nothing?

Weakened, sick, I collapse on the cold ground
I hang my head in harsh, bitter despair
My soul feels the fresh defeat so profound
I'm certain that I'll never recover.

With head on ground, I can't help but observe
A few sticks, dry leaves and other such things
I'm cold, yet not a fire do I deserve
But Desperation forces me to try

The spark shoots up, the gentle flames take hold
I kindle the young fire as if 'twere me
Slowly, then so sudden the fire unfolds
It's a small success...but it's all I have

The flames reach up, sparkling,
and kiss the Dark
I'm surprised, confounded by what I see
For clearly now I can see my path's mark
It's not too late! I can still journey on

Hesitant, but willing, I lift a flare
And peer out at my path clear before me
Truly the answer to my deepest prayer
Inspired, I again begin my walk

My destination lies in unknown space
And so diligently I must traverse
But now the dark is easier to face
Now nothing can stop my forward motion.

I still stumble, I still trip and I fall
Collapsed with fatigue, I still stop to rest
Sometimes I can not walk – that's when I crawl
Pace doesn't matter – just the forward move

I don't know when or how I'll reach my goal
But one thing I'm sure of – it's quite certain
If forward motion I don't stop – my soul
Will eventually find what it's looking for.

A friend of mine once said, "When the sun goes down on your goals, it's time to light a fire," and I loved the visualization. I wrote this poem immediately and sent it to him the following day.

In most poems, it's the second and fourth line that rhyme, but I purposefully chose the 1st and 3rd to rhyme instead. In this way the rhyme is hidden a bit so that the emphasis on rhymes doesn't interrupt the flow of the story-telling.

Remember, life is more like a marathon than a sprint. You may stop to rest; you may see others pass you by; but if you keep putting one foot in front of the other, you will eventually cross the finish line.

Tears of Heaven

The rain pitter patters
on the window and my door—
Tears of heaven crying
Because I cry no more.

And it's eaten me! I'm all hollowed out inside.
And it's beaten me! I can only run and hide!

Tears of heaven falling down...
Rain wash away this hollow empty sound!
Fall on me—wash my soul of this pain!
Fall on me—let me feel once again!

I long since quit my crying—
This pain is just too great.
I long since felt like dying—
This anguish must abate!

I'm a China doll—in this earthquake of pain!
Anytime I'll fall—then I'll never feel again!

Tears of heaven falling down!
Rain wash away this hollow empty sound!
Fall on me—wash my soul of this pain!
Fall on me—let me feel once again!

Once when I was little,
I cried to show my pain,
But after all my screaming—
Life just tortured me again!

Make it over now—no more can I stand
I'm so lonely now—at least stretch out your hand!

Tears of heaven falling down!
Rain wash away this hollow empty sound!
Fall on me—wash my soul of this pain!
Fall on me—let me feel once again!

Fall…fall on me!
Is this…all I can be?
Won't someone hear my prayer…
And send me proof you know I'm here!

Tears of Heaven falling down!
Rain wash away this hollow empty sound!
Fall on me—wash my soul of this pain
And remind me…that I am not insane!

It's forever since I wrote this
…forever since that day
…forever since I felt
My poor soul to decay

But I'm mended now!
I'm not hollow anymore.
I'm transcended now!
It's not what was before!

Tears of heaven falling down,
Now I hear in you a playful, happy sound
Fall on me, I faced my great Unknown
Fall on me, I'm strong enough alone!

One day, in Arizona we had a magnificent monsoon storm. The power, intensity and abruptness fascinated me. I watched the rain fall and heard the thunder rumble and wished that I could do the same. I wanted so much to express my emotions – to tell the world that I was unhappy – but I just couldn't bring myself to say the words.

I no longer need the storms to cry for me, even though I still love them and always will, but this poem is dedicated to all those who do, in the hopes that someday you will be able to speak your own words and cry your own tears.

You Can do Anything!

You can do anything you want to,
If you really want to do it.
You could fly around the world,
If you set your mind right to it.

Though others may deride you,
And do their best to boo it;
You can do anything you want to,
If you really want to do it.

One day while talking of my life—
About what wasn't right,
Was told that if I thought I could—
Or couldn't, I was right.

So heed this gentle wisdom,
And take it through the night—
Though fears are dark they vanish—
When faced with Inner Light.

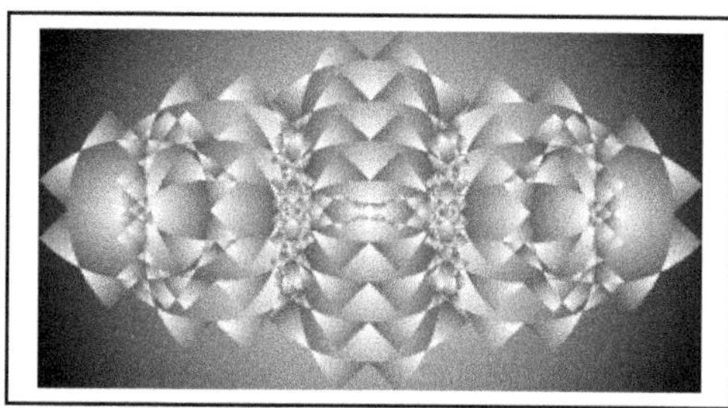

I still remember that day clearly. My family was taking a trip to visit grandparents and the conversation had turned to the idea of, "I can't".

My dad immediately replied, "you can do anything you want to if you really wanna do it". There was a rhythm to the words that caught me, but of course as a child, I had to immediately test the theory.

Soon, my brother and I were coming up with more and more outrageous things that we said were impossible – but his answer never budged. If we wanted it badly enough, we'd find a way to make it happen.

Over the years he said that phrase over and over, and it became a natural part of my personality. A few years ago I thought it was strange that such an important phrase in my life hadn't been turned into a poem, so I wrote this down. It only took a few minutes.

It's message is simple but true – when you truly want something, you will stop at nothing to get it. Often, however, we only want to want it – we don't quite have the gumption to go all the way.

So talk yourself into wanting your goals even more. Talk yourself into making it happen, and may the word "impossible" never find its way into your vocabulary.

Pain Born of Absence

Pain born of absence twists the knife Fate
threw;
I yearn to throw myself into the abyss now—
Swim in darkness, never working it through;
To give up for lack of that dear meow.

My soul cries to cry alone all my days,
To wallow in the mud of this anguish.
If never I can meet his gentle gaze,
Then forever will I sit and languish.

All day and night my mind is filled with hurt,
Analyzing agonizing memories.
I feel to blame—I'm worse than poisoned dirt!
A single thought and I'm brought to my knees.

His dish sits empty, litter box unused,
Bed he slept on lies alone in my room.
Never can I forgive this pain—I'm bruised;
My very soul by agony consumed.

Some say "move on, live your life, let go,"
But they can not possibly understand,
The smallest glance of him set my soul aglow!
More than myself—I felt important...grand.

This pain is far, far, far too much to bear.
I've died inside a thousand times this hour!
I eat in misery, I breathe in despair,
No more doubt now, I will be devoured.

Such Darkness is a most welcome relief
From pain of loss, my never-ending grief.

And then...
The smallest flash of peace creeps inside me...
Thoughts of time we shared and the
lessons learned.
A moment later peace becomes my banshee,
Despair familiar threatens to return.

So do I choose to work for inner peace?
To push myself toward some resolution?
Or choose I instead to refuse release?
Give into pain instead of solution?

Perhaps the grief has won, I've gone insane,
Resisting the sweet, peaceful letting go—
I choose instead to walk beside my pain.
I just don't care whether or not I'll grow.

My child is gone; a piece of me is torn.
I am lost, forever damned by this past!
It's more than it is possible to mourn...
Of all my terrors, this is unsurpassed.

And yet...

I can not seem to stop it, like my breath,
Instinctual, like a heartbeat it comes...
It's quite the torture, worthy of Macbeth—
Forced into slavery: weak, bereft and numb.

I fight and fight to remain in the dark—
The bright world seems horrifically profane!
But something inside me resists this mark,
Forces me back to a happy domain...

How can such loss be ever forgotten?
How can I simply move on and let go?
Nature forbids your soul to be rotten,
Thus this tortuous gift we did bestow.

Take it back! I beg! I plead and I pray!
No longer hold me hostage to your goals.
You're born to greatness, you can't go astray;
Your Destiny demands your very soul.

And though you cry and do regret this speech,
One day, you'll look back and you <u>will</u>
feel peace.
But I want to give up—it's within reach!
Just let me go and from this Fate I'll cease.

There are those who choose their Fate
in their time,
Whose acts decide the course Destiny walks.
You chose your path, before or hence:
your climb—
It does no good to tantrum at the clock.

But no one understands my pain so hard!
If I quickly heal, they understand less.
My heart, my soul, my being: all now scarred—
And this is what you want to call progress?

A muscle grows through microscopic tears.
In opposition, always do we grow.
We all get hurt, and then become aware.
Even in the depths of pain, this you know.

I'm ill prepared for such lofty thoughts now,
I still feel that I am the one to blame.
You have all the time you need, this I vow;
Try to keep absolution as your aim.

I can not keep going,
My pain is still growing.
I force my hands to cease...
And hope I've said my piece.

Yet even as I end I know I'm a fighter,
And that thought alone...makes me feel lighter.

I have a very special relationship with one of my cats. He can always bring a smile to my face no matter how stressed, tired or anxious I might be. Even as I write this he walked up and meowed at me.

One day he went missing and I began staying up at nights to watch for him at the patio door. The days passed by and my natural optimism began to falter. Weeks passed, and I fell into deep grief. I felt I'd never know joy again and wondered if after all I'd been through, if this is what would finally break me.

Months passed by, and eventually I came to realize that just as a plant can't help but absorb water and sunlight, I could not help but fight. It's what I am, not what I sometimes do.

I knew then that I would recover, that it may forever leave a cat-shaped scar on my heart, but I would heal around it and know love again. That was the happy ending to this poem.

Luckily for me, there was another happy ending when my cat's microchip allowed me to bring him home once more. Several months had passed, but he's here with me again.

I dedicate this poem to those who can not help but fight—even when they yearn to give up, they keep putting one foot in front of the other. May you never cease…

One more try

I have come from the land of sorrow,
I have been through the lands of pain.
I have felt my poor heart go hollow,
I have suffered it all again.

Yet the spring comes,
The flowers bloom,
And my aching heart,
Finds it has room...

For one more try - I'll say goodbye,
And though I cry - still on I try!
Just one more try - one try to find
My soul at peace - my peace of mind.
Just one more try!

I have watched as my whole world crumbled,
I have seen where it all will end.
I have know what it is to stumble,
I have been there again and again.

And you're searching for another spring,
And you're waiting for what it will bring,
But it feels just like a fairy tale,
Where it's all made up...it's never real!

Just one more try - though you may die,
And wonder why - just on I try!
Just one more try - one try to see
The beauty that - is inside me.
Just one more try!

Now the trouble here, within this rhyme,
Is we only learn in our own time
And though others may beseech and cry,
It's up us...just one more try!

Just one more try – you're on your own,
No waiting here - future unknown!
Just one more try - it's all there is.
The answer to - Life's little quiz...
Is: one more try!

It was the first part of 2008 and I had a mystery illness that seemed to progress rapidly without anyone able to diagnose it. With no relief in sight, my thoughts turned to the themes of my life. I felt the overwhelming pain that had been ever-present and my tenacious ability to keep going.

This poem is really a song, and it was my theme song during a time when I thought, perhaps, I'd met my end. Fortunately, it was not the case, and that One More Try led, this time, to a new life.

<u>A Stranger's Smile</u>

I wander the country, through towns and
through cities,
I can't stay for long in one place.
I carry a guitar and sing my small ditties,
I see people's scorn in their face.

From city to city I walk all day long,
Unless people give me a lift.
I tell them my story, I sing them my song,
It's all that I have as a gift.

I forage in dumpsters, I sleep in the shelters,
I sit out alone in the night.
Some try to save me from a life helter-skelter,
Others, they just want a fight.

Alone in the world, alone in my mind,
My heart is filled with pain.
All for the lack of somebody kind
To help me feel again.

A shadow am I, and nobody cares,
Under the stars I cry.
I'm certain that I haven't a prayer—
It's time to say goodbye.

I cry as I climb up to the bridge,
Certain that I am damned.
No one will notice—not even a smidge.
Oh! What a wretch I am!

I heave my guitar over the edge,
And stare at the passing cars.
Dirt am I—no—worse, dredge—
Nothing but a mar.

Time seems to stop as a van passes by,
Inside I see a child.
She looks at me—straight in the eye—
Miraculously she smiles.

She smiled at me…she smiled at me!
In wonder is my mind.
My heart begins to fill with glee—
Why would she be kind?

I stare back at the passing car
To see her looking back.
She shall be my shining star,
Whenever my heart lacks.

I heave my guitar back to me,
I set my burdens down.
From this day on I know I'll be
At peace and never frown.

I walk away and leave those things,
My path before my eyes.
And finally my heart can sing,
The old frustration dies.

I'll begin a life, I'll get a job,
My joy I will create.
From this day on—no more slob;
My future now awaits.

Time has passed, as time oft will,
But that young one's smile
Bolsters me on my path still,
And haunts me all the while.

I now have money, I now have fame,
I have a lovely wife.
But still she haunts me, still the same—
That girl that changed my life.

The little girl got up from sleep
And went outside to play.
Daddy! Mommy! Can we keep?
The pony answered, "neigh".

A note attached to pony dear—
They read it in surprise,
And then they smiled from ear to ear—
Tears welling in their eyes.

"Thank you for the tender smile—
you changed my life that day.
Now I can do something worthwhile;
So come on out and play."

While driving in the city one day I happened to see a homeless man on an overpass and my imagination began to run wild with possible futures for him. Suddenly this poem began to come to mind, but I wasn't sure what it was that would save the man in my poem.

Just then, some kids in the back of a minivan in front of me waved and smiled. I smiled and waved back, remembering such antics myself. I realized that sometimes all it takes is a simple smile to bring someone back from the brink.

I've often written about the power we have as strangers – how a compliment goes further, a smile seems brighter, and all because we didn't know the person – and thus this poem was born. This one is dedicated to everyone who takes the time to smile at strangers.

Forever a Canvas

While we are in a person's life,
It's our responsibility
To paint their life with happiness,
And joy and sensitivity.

So that long after we have left
Their lives for other, newer climes;
The Joyful colors left behind
Gently remind them of those times.

Our lives are a painting
And each of us apply
Colors of emotion, esteem…
Until we say goodbye.

My painting is a myriad piece
With colors dark and bright.
Some colors—painful to remember
But covered with Joyful light.

For some have painted
On my canvas with such care—
Carefully covered painful portions—
Answers to my prayers.

As slowly colors build upon
My lifelong canvas true,
I see the glimmer of a trend
In each new sparkling hue.

Before, my canvas was darkly filled—
Forsaken, filled with pain and grief.
And now I start to see the colors
Of happiness, joy, beauty and relief.

Let's use our paintbrushes with great care,
And take the time to color well.
For long after we are gone,
Our colors stay there still.

Each one of us is and always will be,
Forever a Canvas, an artistry.
So great care should be granted,
With our brushes Enchanted,
To always leave behind
The most beautiful colors of our mind.

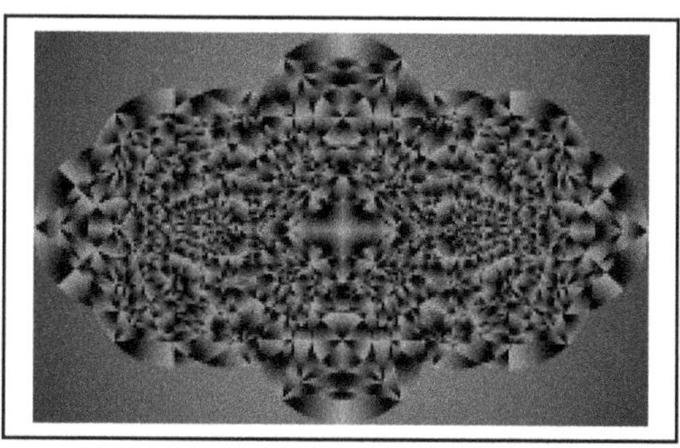

In the early part of 2010 a friend said to me, “While we are in a person’s life it is our responsibility to paint their life with enough joy to color their memories of us after we have departed.” It instantly inspired this poem.

As it all took shape in my mind, I was entranced by the idea of us each being a canvas. Some of our paintings are done mostly by others and some mostly by ourselves. Some are chaotic, some structured and some have been painted over and over.

It occurred to me that if I had a particular dark and dreary section on my canvas, that perhaps someone else could come along and paint a bright spot over the top of it. What a magnificent idea!

Not only do we paint each other’s canvases, but we have the ability to help those around us to overcome the painful parts of their lives as we paint over them with friendship and acceptance.

This poem is dedicated to all those who take great care on how they paint the canvases around them.

Scars

Just because you can't see my scars
Doesn't mean they are not there.
I feel their stiffness, I feel their pain
They are with me everywhere.

I'm filled with envy, perhaps jealousy
Of those with scars more easy to see,
For few understand the pain that I feel—
Few comprehend, and few see it as real.
Fewer still know just what to say
When confronted by scars that won't melt away.

And so I write and think and Dream
Of a world where I am what I seem:
An Optimist with a passion for living,
Filled with Kindness and a spirit for giving;
A woman whose eyes sparkle and smile,
Laughing my way though Life all the while.

Perhaps these scars will melt away
...Though never faced the light of day.
Perhaps...in time, the smooth skin you see
Will match the peace inside of me.

So many scars aren't visible to the eye, and while sometimes that's handy, sometimes it can make it harder to heal or to understand those around you. Imagine how much simpler it would be if we all had visual cues about what hurts people held inside – but then that creates its own set of problems.

I have Somatization Disorder, which basically means that the emotional scars I have manifest themselves in strange physical ways. For years I haven't been able to walk normally, and there's no physical reason.

Sometimes I wish I had some kind of visible problem so people would know that if I'm on my feet, I shouldn't be there for long. Sometimes I wish I had a physical issue so it wouldn't be so hard to explain. Sometimes I'm grateful because it's much easier to hide this.

When it all boils down, we all wish we were seen for who we really are instead of the fleeting parts that seem to catch the eye. We don't want to be known for our age or race or handicap; we want to be known for who we are as a person.

I have great hope that one day I'll recover from my illness, but I'm flexible. Perhaps I'll just learn to be comfortable in the body I have. That would be pretty special too.

See Beyond the Pain

Time rolls slowly on;
we can not halt its gentle spin.
It tumbles on, like a dime, forever true.
Pain was always there;
it came before us in the womb,
It leads the way, from Night to Day,
against our Will.

See beyond the Pain!
Live that you may grow!
Past to Future—one small trend,
Learn that you may know!

What now have you learned
from this experience?
How can you use it in your life
to shape your future?
Learning takes away that dreadful
Pain in the Darkness.
Knowledge takes the present to the future!

See beyond the Pain!
Live that you may grow!
Past to Future—one small trend,
Learn that you may know!

What now can it mean,
This small dot in eternity?
Unless you let it grow
Inside your heart.
Use this tiny dot
To help you shape your future.
Use the Pain inside
To make you strong!

See beyond the Pain!
Live that you may grow!
Past to Future—one small trend,
Learn that you may know!

Though we do not wish it,
will it, want it in our lives,
Still it will come –
it's our companion
through our lifetime.
Learn to lose your fear,
and it will lose its deadly hold,
Build your courage strong and it will fade!

See beyond the Pain!
Live that you may grow!
Past to Future—one small trend,
Learn that you may know!

I wrote this, originally a song, in high school while I was going through a particularly rough period. Most people will refer to their teenage years as rough, but this was especially so.

One day, while sitting in the back seat of the family car, I felt the urge to write, since it had always been my escape. The problem was, I couldn't figure out what I should write about.

I decided to try to blank my mind and then write about the very first thing that came to me. As soon as I began, I saw an image in my mind's eye of a dime spinning on a tabletop.

My mind flooded with possible directions: heads or tails; dimes are the smallest coin; dimes are 10 cents and we live in a base 10 world. There were so many ideas to choose from, but as I stared at that image in my mind, what occurred to me the strongest was the idea that two different things are sometimes referred to as, "different sides of the same coin".

Perhaps the pain I lived in and the joy I desired were two sides of that coin. Perhaps that dime would spin forever and never rest. Perhaps it would only spin for an instant, and few would know the magic it had held. What does the spinning dime hold for you?

I used to Soar with Eagles

I used to soar with Eagles high above.
I knew respect and fame, and I knew love;
But then – catastrophe! I could not fly!
I pumped my wings but something was awry.

With deep despair I headed to the ground—
Lay there broken…battered…
my wounds profound.
I fought to look up to the sky I knew
My gentle heart just shattered at the view.

For how could I e're hope to fly away,
When battered, broken, on the ground I lay.
My wounds too great, my pain
too fierce, I cried!
I thought 'twould be better if I had died.

I lay there bleeding, I know not how long,
But one day woke to a beautiful song.
I lifted my head to see who was there,
But no one around that I was aware.

Again I slept to avoid the drear sight
Of my Eagle friends flying in the light.
Again I woke to that pure, simple tune.
I had *to find that music's source – and soon.*

I looked around for one who might have seen
The maker of that sound, sweet & serene.
I spied a mouse in a hovel near me
And said, "Please, whose is
that sweet melody?"

That mouse looked at me with a look so queer…
"That's your song of course that has
filled your ear."
"Now please, Mr. Mouse, I'm sure you can see
I'm in no shape to sing such melody."

"In shape or not, it's your song you have heard,
And why wouldn't you sing? You are a bird."
"But I'm broken," said I,
"and should be dead."
"Only bones break, not a spirit," *he said.*

"Your spirit is stronger than you believe;
You only lay here so that you can grieve;
But when your not thinking about your pain…
You're spirit rises and sings once again."

I stared at that mouse – his words felt so true!
And yet, I was scared to again pursue
The great blue sky, waiting…waiting above.
I was so scared to pursue love.

"Okay Mr. Mouse, if it's as you say,
I'll stretch out a wing and sing straightaway."
I stretched – surprised 'twas stiff
but not too sore.
Was it possible that I'd fly once more?

I took a deep breath and began to sing—
The music surrounded my soul like Spring!
I began to get up, my legs still pained,
But who would need legs
with wings unrestrained?

Still quite nervous of those beckoning heights,
I kept myself to the safe, lower lights;
But once again, when not thinking I'd find
Myself way up high – so free – unconfined!

And now, much later, I tell you this tale.
The heights are my home now, I have prevailed.
I needed time to heal my wounds inside...
I'm so grateful now that I didn't die.

That mouse is my friend, he helped me to see
That the cure I so needed – was just me.
It was I that sang myself back to be
A high flying bird, enraptured and free.

While perusing through Facebook, I read a comment from a man who was tired of having to get up after so many falls. It was clear that life had given him a hard time, and he felt tired of the struggle to feel whole again. How well I understood!

I felt such a well of emotions that I knew I had to write. What else may be afraid of falling? High flying eagles, of course.

The first six stanzas came immediately. Only a few minutes had passed, but then I was stuck. What would pull him back up again? I thought and thought and was just about to ask the question on the same Facebook page that had started it all, but even as I considered asking it I realized what my reply would have been if I'd seen the question. The best hero of all would be the eagle himself. He would sing himself back to flight.

The line, "*who would need legs with wings unrestrained?*" is my favorite because, like my eagle friend, I can not walk well. Like him, I dream of flying and one day my legs will either heal or I won't need them anymore.

Sometimes all we need is a casual observer, someone removed from our situation to look at us with the scrutiny of a mouse and tell us the truth. Sometimes, like with a mouse to an eagle – it comes in surprising places.

<u>Rippled Reflections</u>

Water reflects…& I reject
the vision I see—it is not me!
Its ripples & waves leave me depraved.
My soul sends a plea—please let it not be me!

It's weird and distorted,
And must be aborted.
These lies I will flee—
But it must be me…

My soul hears a whisper as a peaceful breeze,
"Beware of reflections, don't give in to these."
"For how can you trust a mirror so flawed?
'Tis dupery I say—this imposter is fraud!"

I protest the voice, "do not my mind prey!
for this Water is people & I hear what they say!"

"People are imperfect, a well proven fact.
'Tis crazy to deny it & worse to react."
"For how can a flaw tell what is true?
How can imperfection show the real you?"

Becalmed now, I slowly agree.
This rippled reflection is not the real me.
And since not a person is a mirror ideal,
I'll just have to trust the way that I feel.

Once again it was a Facebook comment that led to this poem. A woman had written that she felt like everyone judged her negatively. Others, including myself, tried to convince her otherwise, but to my knowledge, she never replied.

I wrote this poem thinking of her, thinking of so many others and thinking of myself. It's difficult when the only mirrors we have around us are flawed, but we have to remember that they're not true mirrors – they're people. They're people with troubles and insecurities all their own, and they don't usually reflect accurately.

What tremendous courage it takes to step out of the darkness in our mind and judge ourselves by ourselves, rather than what we've been told by others. I applaud everyone who attempts it, and I sincerely congratulate those who have succeeded.

I humbly dedicate this poem to all those who have this courage – the courage to continuously try to see who they really, really are and not who someone says they are. Keep up the effort – the prize is worth it.

Do Not Mistake Me

Do not mistake me for yourself;
Do not mistake me for my mother.
I am my own being, none other.

Though you may think these things are similar,
They really can not be.
Common things of past and present
Are at best, a novelty.

My life is mine, and you do not know
What roads I have trod.
Nor can I know what troubles you faced—
Such things are only for God.

So keep silent, my friend, and try to hear
What my actions say.
Instead of seeing yourself, I ask
That you look to another day.

I love you, dearest friend,
You're strange, but good.
I just need you to see me…as me,
And let me be understood.

We've all had those moments when we felt the advice we were being given was better suited to the person giving it than to ourselves. This was written as a response to one of those situations, though I never showed it to them.

In life we're often unfairly compared to others. To me, it's a simple reminder that each of us is our own individual and even when small portions of our lives may seem similar to those around us, it doesn't mean that the rest of our lives will follow their path.

We all have our own lives to lead and deserve to be seen as such. This poem is dedicated to those who are brave enough to forge their own path, without letting other people's ideas define them.

Standing on the Precipice

I'm standing on the Precipice,
Staring deep into the Abyss.
Darkness falls…
I give my All…
But I'm just a screaming shadow.

I want so much to make my home,
To settle down and not to roam,
but Starvation is a deadly key
That forces action out of me.

I'm standing on the Precipice,
And nothing seems to matter.
I'm Alice in my Wonderland—
My God is the Mad Hatter.

Perhaps another future waits—
Perhaps Starvation can abate.
But for me to choose that plate—
This Darkness must get sated.

I'm standing on the Precipice,
Staring deep into the Abyss.
I want the courage to run and leap—
To fill my soul with gladness deep—
but Courage is a cost too steep.

A wonder true, 'tis strange to tell—
How someone can stand by in hell,
Instead of going to future bright…
All because the Change is blight.

But Change is Life and Life is Change,
All the world gets Rearranged;
But in the chaos of my mind
I can't move on, though t'would be kind.

And so I stand and, looking down,
I see my soul—it wears a frown.
Where's the gumption? Self-esteem?
Where's the light? Where's the gleam?

Can I jump? I do not know…
Even if my joy lies down below.
My own Self is my darkest foe…
But if I jump, then I will grow.

My heart beats fast, my lungs breathe deep—
What sort of future could <u>I</u> reap?
What if the cost is much too steep?
Dare I take this last big leap?

Looking back at stable ground,
I remember the last time that I found
Myself in this position…

I remember the fear and the glee,
Remember the joy at what would be.
I remember the sorrow at leaving behind…
Was a tiny price for the joy that I'd find.

But I thought that was this time
And that this time was last!
I thought that I was settled
Back there in the past!
I thought I was done…
But I'm beginning again!
Oh! What is this doing
To my struggling brain!

I look down below at the cliff at my feet.
I wonder if I this darkness can beat.
Is there a choice? Or is my life not mine?
Do I surrender and say, "my will be thine?"
I've done it before, I'll do it again,
But can my heart take it? Or is it too stained?

I'm Standing on the Precipice,
Staring deep into the Abyss…

…

This poem can not finish,
Not 'til I decide
Whether I'll take that big leap—
Or run back and hide.

We've all faced those difficult moments when we're forced to change our lives dramatically, and this was written during one such time. Ultimately the choice was still mine but the pressures were high.

Worse, it seemed that I had been through all this before – that history had repeated itself and I was frustrated at the prospect of starting all over again.

Ultimately, though, we play the hand we're dealt, right? I had to face that decision and choose whether or not to take that big leap or hide in a shell. Everyone at some point makes the same big decisions.

Here I sit, years later, and I'm grateful I jumped, though part of me will always wonder, "what if?" To this day parts of this poem go round in my mind when I face challenges, and it helps me, as I hope it helps you.

Pain

The minutes tick by
like hours in my mind—
An hour passes and it feels like a day!
Help and support
I yearn to find—
But there simply isn't a way.

Sometimes we're forced to face a hell
And deal with it on our own.
How I wish I could have
a hug right now...
Instead of being alone.

Alone am I, alone am I...
Just a single solitary soul.
And all I see, all I see...
Are things that stop me
from being whole.

I wish I could remove this pain,
But it seems it's not Fate's will.
I wish I could feel good again!
...Perhaps after I climb this hill.

I've tried to run,
I've tried to hide—
I've tried to stuff it all inside.
But it didn't stay—
Didn't go away.
Only festered and pussed—
Only whimpered and fussed.

So I'll bring it now to the light of day,
Hoping the sun will drive the shadows away.
It hurts…oh! It hurts!
But I've had pain before,
And maybe…just maybe…
I can heal this once more.

Yes, I understand the kind of long term, numbing pain that feels it's rotting your soul. I know what loneliness is, and I know what helplessness feels like.

The strange beauty of it is that everyone knows these feelings – so the very act of feeling them means you're not alone!

Over and over I've found that shadows are darkest when the lights are off. The mental demons that haunt us get smaller once we shine a light on them and look them in the eye.

Try it sometime; I dedicate this poem to all those who do.

Drifting

Drifting…
High above an emotional sea.
Numb…
As though none of it really is me.

I watch myself
As I go through life,
With an eerie calm—
No joy, no strife.

'Tis not the calm
Of a winter's night,
With a crackling fire
And your lover in sight.

It is instead
the calm of the dead;
And I don't know why—
but I can not cry!

What lies trapped
Inside my heart?
When will I live
And play a part?

These are the things
I surely <u>must</u> know!
Else I am stagnant—
A mildewed soul.

So here at the end,
I wonder these things.
But all I can do is wait…
…And see what the waiting brings.

At the tender age of 25 I was already going through a divorce, and this experience seemed to find every little weakness inside of me and exploit it. I was numb with the emotions of it all, and remember feeling cut off from life, distant from living and not knowing if I'd ever feel again.

I did learn to feel again, but it meant being willing to dive head first into that emotional sea and surrender myself to the storm. Who would choose pain if you could choose something else? Sadly, it's the only way to free yourself from that numbness and move on to happier feelings.

To all those who read this, I sincerely hope that when such storms face you, you have the courage to dive in head first and face your inner storms. Just remember to lean on your friends and come up for air every now and then.

Changes

I don't really know
What it is that I feel—
A thousand emotions
Make my head reel!

New thoughts—new ideas—
New ambitions—new goals.
My entire life is changing—
Clear down to my soul!

Sink or swim? I'll swim away!
Water I will not tread.
Holding still or going down—
Just other forms of being dead.

I'll climb the mountain's highest heights!
With Eagles I will soar!
Each obstacle becomes a stepping stone—
Each barrier—a door!

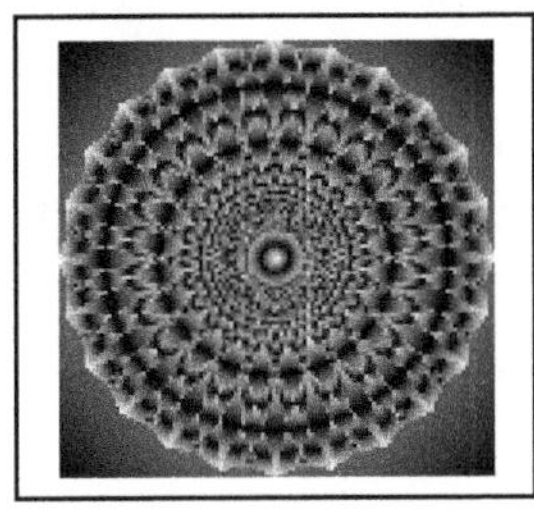

It's fitting that this poem, Changes comes immediately after Drifting, since that's how they were written.

After the numbness and waiting and stagnation in the previous poem I threw myself into my inner storms and faced them down. Perhaps it was due to my youth, perhaps mere circumstance but it seemed to all go away so fast, and very quickly I had good things to feel.

It's strange, isn't it? When we feel bad we long to feel good, and yet if it comes too fast it can leave us reeling, desperate to keep up. This is how I felt when I wrote Changes.

My life was spinning, and I felt something like Alice when she first encountered Wonderland – trying so hard to make sense of emotions that never could make sense at all.

In the end all I knew is that I had to keep moving forward – or at least keep moving when I didn't know which direction "forward" was.

True to my youth, I felt ready to conquer mountains and blindly felt that the worst was behind me, but the part of this poem that has stuck with me the most is the third verse. Those 22 simple words have echoed in my mind every time life deals a harsh blow, reminding me that as long as I keep swimming, eventually I'm bound to reach a shore.

I Have To / I Want To

I have to work and pay the bills,
I have sleep and take my pills,
I have to exercise each day,
I have to watch how much I weigh.

I have to wash the dishes now,
So many worries on my brow,
Like accidents on highway three,
And what about the economy?!

I wake up early, make my bed,
Get dressed up and hold my head,
It aches with all there is to do--
Oh no! I think the bills are due!

I feel I'm spinning out of control,
With all my many, many roles,
Check my email, Facebook too,
There are so many things to do.

****

S*it down! Desist!*
T*ake a break!*
O*bstacles will wait.*
P*lease…for your sake.*
****

Breathe in...breathe out...
Feel surroundings all about.
Breathe out...breathe in...
Relaxing never was a sin.

Exhale...and let the world renew...
Inhale...and reacquaint with you.
Slowly breathing...take in air...
Then let it out...with all your cares.

Renewed, refocused, recharged, reborn--
After midnight's stress, it's Soul's new morn.
Relaxed, recouped, relieved, remade--
I sing myself a serenade.

Open eyes, now primed to see
My central goals – priorities;
Ready now to face my day,
Ready now without delay.

Another look at chores to do...
With new eyes, let's now review...

I am glad that I'm employed
And healthy body I enjoy
I want to exercise each day
And grateful I have dishes – yay!

I want to drive and pay my bills
I want my life with all its thrills
It's funny how much my life has changed
Since this simple thought was rearranged.

So heed this simple wisdom, dear,
And don't feel overthrown
By 'musts' and 'haves' and
'shoulds' and such...
Keep yourself in that zone...

****

Just Remember...

When I had to –
T'was bad to
But when I want –
It's nonchalant!

I had just finished my first meeting with a prestigious Life Coach and thought about what sh said. I realized that I was so focused on all the “shoulds” in my life that I wasn’t really getting anything done at all. I was so frantically spinning wheels, that I’d lost my forward motion.

I sat down to think, opened up my journal a began writing, putting my thoughts and feelings in words - and as they so often do, they came out in poetic form.

It was important to me, as I wrote this poem that it have some of that frenetic energy in the first section. Sometimes we get so lost in such rhythms that we lose track of the melody. I knew I needed t STOP, making for a fun segue to the next section.

I sat on my recliner, writing all this in my journal and allowed myself to just breathe, which le to writing about breathing.

Once I’d breathed a bit, I remembered my Grandma who always enjoyed doing dishes because meant there had been food to eat. I took some time remember how lucky I am to have what I do, and th in itself helped me to refocus on the bigger picture i my life.

That coaching session and this poem were what finally led to the creation of this book. Becaus of that I sincerely dedicate this poem to that wonderful Life Coach and wish her the utmost success in all her endeavors.

First time at the Rose Gardens

It's often been said
By those who are dead
That a rose by any other name
Would smell as sweet – 'twould be the same.

Yet in this garden of flowers bright,
My mind plays tricks with color and light;
And surrounded by angelic sight,
I feel myself grow stronger in might.

The roses are planted, then bloom and die.
Understanding of such is not for I.
Their thorns may be many,
Their thorns may be few,
Understanding of such is not for you.

As I walk among rows of colorful gems,
I'm struck by the contrast
'Tween flower and stem.
The stem – such a strong and powerful beast,
The rose feels not threatened – not in the least.

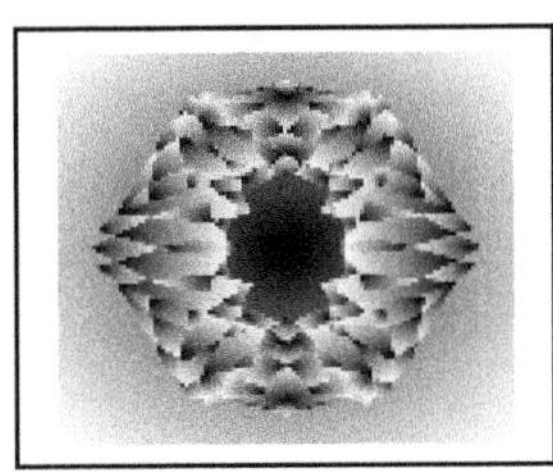

A bride wanders in – resplendent in gown
As lovely as all the flowers around.
A photographer snaps the pictures
And off the party goes;
And another bride enters –
The joy of her day shows.

As people gently mill and wander all about,
I find it hard to worry, frown or even pout.
These flowers create such a peaceful place,
I can not help but echo their grace.

This garden is a blessed glade
Where Heaven and Flora meet.
So I walk awhile, relax awhile,
And breathe the air so sweet.

Portland, Oregon, is home to the world renowned Rose Gardens. Tier after tier of prize winning roses decorate the landscape, making it a popular place for weddings and other photographic moments.

I was first amazed and then entranced by the sweet smell, the colors and the peacefulness of that place. It's a mind transforming experience, and if you can't make it there, just look at a rose – really look – and let yourself go. I think you'll understand what I mean.

Still the Trees Grow

People and buildings, they come and they go,
We fret and we worry our minds to and fro.
Still…the trees grow.
Still…the trees grow.

We fear for our death, We fear for our life,
We fight with each other in turmoil and strife.
Still…there is life.
Still…there is life.

The Oak tree stands; the Willow still flows;
The water laps up; the wind still blows.

The sounds of Eternity
Linger on still,
Whether or not
Our own minds will.

The porpoise's laughter
Still welcome the Dawn;
The mother doe nurses
Her own little fawn.

Still the trees grow; Still there is strife;
Still there is joy; Still there is life.

I grew up in the desert and have always found it a wonderful analogy to my life. It's a harsh place, to be sure, and the plants and animals respond in their own harshness. Yet there is much more life there than most people realize. Most see the desert as empty and void of life, but quite the opposite is true. It simply waits for the rain to fall.

I had a birthday coming up, which always puts me in a philosophical mood. Suddenly I realized in a flash that if I ceased to exist, the desert would go on unchanged. I broadened my perspective and thought of earthquakes, fires, floods – all of it could come and go and the desert would go on.

Life is far tougher than we give it credit for, and this poem is for all those who understand that. The trees will grow, life will move forward. In the end, life just moves along, and I find it much simpler to move with it than against it.

So find the natural rhythms around you. Settle into them and see where the patterns take you. Even the most parched life, like the deserts I wandered as a child, has beauty and hope hidden in the crevices.

She was Divine

A Loneliness crept quietly,
Sneaking up her spine—
Perceptive, she stopped it,
For She was Divine.

So Emptiness came rushing past,
Trying to catch her in its wake.
But Awareness was Hers to hold—
She knew the Emptiness a Fake.

Then came Grief and Sadness
And their secret weapon: Regret,
But She was filled with Light and Love,
With only Joy to beget.

Frustration left with all the rest,
Without a word to say.
She? She kept on smiling—
Oblivious they'd been there that day.

When I wrote this poem I was going through yet another particularly difficult period in my life, and I wondered how it would be possible to ever escape turmoil when so much of it seemed to come from outside my own life.

I had done so much to try to rise above such problems, but they seemed to always find a way in, and I was desperate for an answer.

I imagined a woman who was so in tune with herself, so much in the habit of meeting her own needs that her subconscious would handle the issues while she went along through life, hardly aware they had touched her.

Oh she's still there to comfort those in need, aware of the problems in the world – but the internal struggles such things often trigger are met so naturally that she seldom ever notices them.

What a joy it would be to become her! To know how to nourish the positive aspects in my soul and to create habits that weed the bad parts out, to become a self-repairing individual - yes, that would be a real joy to accomplish.

That concept is still my goal, and the mere presence of the goal helps me on some of the harder days. I try to imagine how this woman might handle things, and I do what I can to copy it. I hope the visual works for you, too.

Conclusion

Out of the Darkness…The title itself assumes you're in the dark, and yet you are not. It often feels that way, to be sure, but the light is already within you to see your way to a new freedom and a new happiness.

Our light often gets buried underneath the stresses, traumas and anxieties of life, but it's always there. Trust in that fact, and work to find your own inner light. After all, it's far easier to find something that you believe exists.

This book was written with a great deal of emotion won from countless situations both positive and negative. I've seen much in this life, and it's given me a unique perspective that seems to benefit others. I don't know how I got it, but it's proven true, and I trust it now.

My most sincere wish is that you, the reader, will find something amidst these words that helps you to see your life differently, that helps you to find opportunities for growth and helps you find the inner peace that so many of us are searching for.

If, in the end, I have accomplished this, then I feel even more at peace in my own life, since I've dedicated myself to comforting the disturbed and to disturbing the comfortable.

So whether I have given you comfort or forced you to see the world around you in a different light, either way I have reached my success and I thank you for your part in it.

Life is a funny little thing,
One moment is cold – the next is Spring.
A reminder to be Grateful,
Never being hateful,
For paupers may become Kings.

It's true that life is filled with contradictions and fast changes that can be hard to keep up with; but I believe that if we're always true to ourselves, if we are patient with ourselves and if we remember that the future is unknown and may be filled with amazing thing; then I believe we will eventually find our happiness.

Keep your forward motion, soar with Eagles and never be ashamed to admit your own greatness. *See beyond the pain* in your life, and with practice it may show you that:

Each obstacle becomes a stepping stone—
Each barrier—a door!

~Cyleste Farnsworth

www.ingramcontent.com/pod-product-compliance
Ingram Content Group UK Ltd.
Pitfield, Milton Keynes, MK11 3LW, UK
UKHW020217250726
13967UKWH00001B/58

9 780557 940134